Google Classroom

A Beginner's Guide to Online Teaching for Teachers and Students. Get the Best from Distance Learning and Teaching with Google and Learn How to Manage Virtual or Blended Classrooms.

Grace Douglas

Copyright - 2020 -All rights reserved.

The content contained within this book may not be reproduced, duplicated or transmitted without direct written permission from the author or the publisher.

Under no circumstances will any blame or legal responsibility be held against the publisher, or author, for any damages, reparation, or monetary loss due to the information contained within this book. Either directly or indirectly.

Legal Notice:

This book is copyright protected. This book is only for personal use. You cannot amend, distribute, sell, use, quote or paraphrase any part, or the content within this book, without the consent of the author or publisher.

Disclaimer Notice:

Please note the information contained within this document is for educational and entertainment purposes only. All effort has been executed to present accurate, up to date, and reliable, complete information. No warranties of any kind are declared or implied. Readers acknowledge that the author is not engaging in the rendering of legal, financial, medical or professional advice. The content within this book has been derived from various sources. Please consult a licensed professional before attempting any techniques outlined in this book.

By reading this document, the reader agrees that under no circumstances is the author responsible for any losses, direct or indirect, which are incurred as a result of the use of information contained within this document, including, but not limited to, - errors, omissions, or inaccuracies.

TABLE OF CONTENTS

INTRODUCTION	5
CHAPTER - 1 WHAT IS GOOGLE CLASSROOM	11
CHAPTER - 2 GETTING STARTED WITH GOOGLE CLASSROOM	19
CHAPTER - 3 HOW TO MANAGE HOMEWORK AND ASSIGNMENTS	31
CHAPTER - 4 MANAGING CLASSES FOR STUDENTS	43
CHAPTER - 5 GOOGLE DOCS AND GOOGLE SHEETS	57
CHAPTER - 6 INTRODUCING GOOGLE SLIDES IN YOUR CLASSROOM	69
CHAPTER - 7 HIDDEN GOOGLE CLASSROOM FEATURES	77
CHAPTER - 8 HOW GOOGLE DOCS CAN HELP YOU WORK WITH STUDENT	81
CHAPTER - 9 GOOGLE CLASSROOM: AN INTERACTIVE PLATFORM	87

CHAPTER - 10
   GOOGLE CLASSROOM
   TIPS & TRICKS   97

CHAPTER - 11
   TROUBLESHOOTING TIPS   107

CHAPTER - 12
   OTHER WAYS GOOGLE
   CLASSROOM CAN HELP YOU
   SUCCEED   117

CHAPTER - 13
   FAQS ABOUT GOOGLE
   CLASSROOM   125

CONCLUSION   129

INTRODUCTION

Technological development is proliferating rapidly today. Developments have been almost sector-specific. Economics, politics, and education also apply the use of technology. Information technology is one of many tools used by managers to anticipate changes. With the development of IT, many people are making innovations to create IT that can be used to make things easier for other people to do their day-to-day activities, ranging from sending messages, doing assignments, communicating online, searching and shopping online, ordering tickets for events and transportation online, and many others. Therefore, many aspects of human life are influenced by technological developments in information, one of which relates to the learning process in the field of education.

Teachers must be able to use the various technologies, and be able to design, compile, guide, and evaluate student projects. Resources and services must be coordinated with colleagues and other professionals. This new role is challenging and requires a different approach to the career development of teachers.

Distance learning is a mode of education where teachers and students are separated, and learning is carried out through telecommunications systems. Many schools and universities around the world have used and experienced this learning system successfully. Educational technology is rising within the classroom. Teachers and educators must be prepared to interact with this emerging technology, which plays a significant role in learning and involves a wide variety of cognitive skills to integrate educational technology into future curriculum.

Applying education technology improves cognitive skills and characteristics. The role of educators in the teaching process in schools is not the same. Still, it depends on institutional characteristics, teaching and learning concepts, individual experiences, and types of teaching personalities. New technologies will not fundamentally change the role of educators; they will have a significant impact on how different teaching approaches can be applied in radically different technological and organizational environments.

One of the technologies is the internet; it has become an important part of life. Almost all human needs have been met through the internet. The government socializes the internet through training/workshops, offices, kindergarten schools, high schools, and many institutions. The ICT center is used in offices, schools, and institutions. It makes it easier for users to access the information they need. Now, the internet can also be accessed via a mobile phone. It makes things more comfortable and practical. It can be shown that many vendors are making quotes faster and cost-effectively. The consumer base is becoming large, and access to information is becoming faster. Information can be obtained anytime and anywhere. Education is one of the sectors in which information and communication technology is developed. Every year, a large number of educational institutions invest a lot in improving their systems, to bridge the existing technological gaps in the curricula. It gives the impression that technology can have a positive effect on students and teachers, in the teaching and learning process. Teacher-centric learning is no longer appropriate for this generation, so it needs to change to a more student-centric approach, especially for students who have diverse skills.

Students are expected to be more active by using the teacher's learning method. For example, students

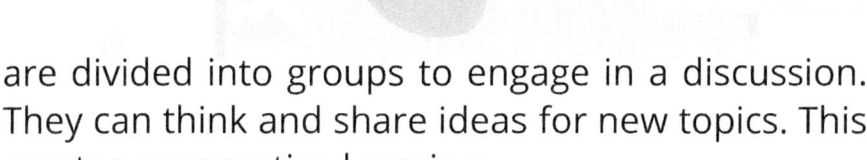

are divided into groups to engage in a discussion. They can think and share ideas for new topics. This creates cooperative learning.

Google Classroom is going to change the essence of instruction. For quite a long time, teachers have spent such an extensive amount of their time, both inside and outside the classroom, attempting to find the most ideal approach to instruct their students and give feedback immediately.

This took long efforts to achieve, and could cut into the learning time for students. To save time, teachers would pick the most effortless alternatives for picking up, removing inventiveness and a portion of the fun in learning.

The hardship was not only for the teacher. Students frequently needed to monitor papers from various classes, and in the confusion, they could mistakenly neglect significant information about the assignments.

Google Classroom has simplified the process in the classroom, and is making communication between teachers and students simpler. Google Classroom does a few things at its heart, and really does them well.

- It provides a central hub for class events.

- It helps teachers to determine assignments (and other classroom activities).
- It collects student assignments.
- It assists teachers in marking assignments and getting reviews.
- It makes giving assignments back to students easier.

CHAPTER - 1
What is Google Classroom

Google Classroom are ease of access, student flexibility in scheduling, and the ability to adapt to work. It has certain valuable functions, such as the simplification of student-teacher interaction, and the ease in distribution and grading of assignments. It allows students to submit their work to their teachers online within the time limit. In the same way, teachers can completely monitor the progress of every student, and they can give the necessary comments to allow the student to revise their assignments. As for students, it provides a Stream of communication and workflow for students. Going paperless is a crucial factor in the development of learning strategies. Hence, students can store their documents more orderly and effortlessly in paperless form in a single program. The teachers' primary task is to enlighten students on how to use the applications. One of the sophistication of this application is that it is also used in a cooperative learning group. The efficient

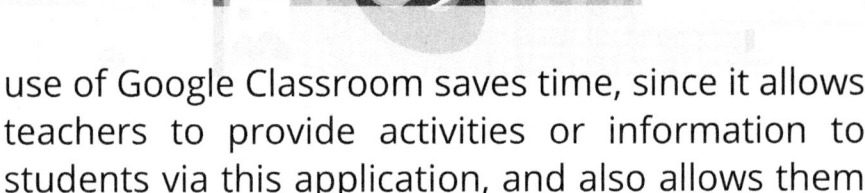

use of Google Classroom saves time, since it allows teachers to provide activities or information to students via this application, and also allows them to upload learning materials.

The Basics of Google Classroom

The capability of Google Classroom to sync with other Google products makes things easier for students and teachers. Communication is done just through regular emails, and it takes just a few seconds for the teacher to create assignments, and for students to submit their work. Also, Google Classroom does not have ads/promotions in the program; hence, no one has to worry about this interfering with the work, or about Google collecting private information.

Assignments

Google Drive is going to be the main point of contact for assignments with Google Classroom. Teachers can either look at documents the students have uploaded, and grade from there, or they can upload a template that each student can change and resubmit as their own. This can be helpful if the teacher needs a worksheet or discussion questions answered for homework. Also, if the student needs to attach supporting documents, this can easily be done in Google Drive as well.

Grading

Teachers can choose the way that they would like to grade on this platform. One option is just to have the students submit the work, and teachers can choose to grade by marking answers before sending the information back. For other assignments, such as projects, and essays, that will take some time, the teacher can track progress, make edits, grade with notes, and send it back for revision.

Several applications can assist with grading as well. Flubaroo is perfect if you have worksheets or multiple-choice tests that simply need to be graded. This application can take the assignment, grade it automatically, and send the grade to the students. Students get feedback right away, even when the teacher is busy.

Communication

Most of the communication can be done through Gmail. Teachers can send announcements, homework assignments, and other information to students. The students can send questions and information back to the teacher when it is most convenient for them. Gmail is easy to use, and it only takes a few minutes for students to create their accounts, if they do not already have one.

GOOGLE CLASSROOM

In addition to using Gmail, Google Drive, and YouTube can be used for communications. Teachers can post new assignments and announcements the students need to Google Drive. YouTube can be great for sending videos and other media, pertaining to the classroom.

Cost and Time

This platform is free to use, for both teachers and students. The teacher simply needs to create their classroom, and then send the class code to their students. This allows the students to attend the class, access any announcements and assignments, and even ask questions. The classroom is secure, so only those invited can see what is inside, and since Google does not allow advertisements, parents know that it is safe.

In addition, the amount of time that teachers can save using this platform is immense. They can add on applications that grade worksheets and homework automatically for them. They will not have to waste time at the copy machine or handing out papers to all the students. They can spend their class time teaching, and save the announcements and homework assignments for later.

Mobile Version

Google has also made a mobile version of Classroom that allows for even more features, including the ability to snap photos and add them to assignments; the ability to share other content including web pages, PDFs, and images; and the ability to get their homework assignments in, even when they are not at home. This is available for both Android and iPhone products, making it easier for everyone to use.

Google Classroom is designed to make education easier. Teachers can spend more time interacting with their students, and less time worrying about all the paperwork. Students can easily get to their important announcements and upload homework assignments timely. With the ability to work with many of the popular Google applications, this is one of the best free platforms to help with education.

Benefits of Google Classroom

In the modern world, there are many similar platforms that promise to deliver success. Google Classroom has many great benefits that the other platforms lack.

- Easy to setup: The setup for Google Classroom only takes a few minutes. The teacher simply needs to set up their class, invite students and

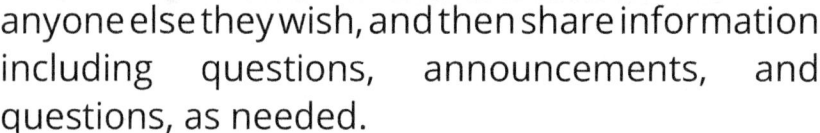

anyone else they wish, and then share information including questions, announcements, and questions, as needed.

- Less paper and time: Instead of teachers making twenty or more copies of each worksheet, or handing out packets of papers for discussions, reading, and tests, all of the work is now online. This can save a lot of paper and makes student management easier.

- Easy organization: Students can join their classroom and see all the assignments in their Work page or on the calendar. The materials needed for the class, such as reading materials, worksheets, and discussion questions, will be located in their Google Drive folder.

- Enhanced communication: Inside Google Classroom, the teacher will be able to release announcements and create assignments. For homework or online classes, discussions can begin in real time. The students can share their resources and interact, even if they are not in the same room.

- Works with other applications: Google Classroom will work with the other Google applications like Forms, Drive, Gmail, Calendar, and Docs, making it easier than ever to complete assignments.

- Secure and affordable: Since this is from Google, the application allows you to keep all of your information secure. There are no advertisements that get in the way, and Google does not use this information to sell advertising space. This makes it secure for students to use. Also, using Google Classrooms is free!

While there are other platforms out there that can help schools with education, Google has many great (and free!) applications that combine into Google Classroom. Since many students are already using these applications, and have a Gmail account or can create one quickly, it is an efficient way to share information between teachers and students. Whether the class takes place in person or is completely online, this is a great resource to save paper, help students get questions answered, and to even promote discussions outside of the classroom.

GOOGLE CLASSROOM

18

CHAPTER - 2
Getting Started with Google Classroom

Before you get started with Google Classroom, here are some important reminders.

- Users can come from various GAFE domains. The IT or administrator can white list the needed domains.

- Apparently, the application seamlessly works with Google Chrome. Although you can use other browsers, not all the features will run smoothly.

- Only the teacher can see all the comments being posted, even deleted ones.

- It has a limit of 1000 students and 100 teachers.

- When using Classroom for the first time as a teacher, select the Teacher option. If not, your administrator will have to reset your account in the Google Applications control panel, to change your role.

- Everyone must be using the same email domain, since they will not be able to join if they use a different domain.

Teachers can add resources and other needed materials such as a syllabuses, classroom rules etc. Select the theme of the class or add a photo in the top section. Again, once you create the class, a Google Drive folder will be automatically created as well. It bears the same title as the name of the class. Assignments and announcements posted will be automatically added to the folder.

Next, the teacher can add or invite students by using the Invite button, after which they can enter the student's email address, or obtain invite codes to hand out to students. The students can enter the class using the code by clicking the (+) button found on the main page.

The teacher can now set commenting rules. Click on the Students can post and comment button, and choose from the available settings.

- No restriction. Basically, they can post and comment, like how they usually would on Facebook.

- Students can only comment on the teacher's post, or only the teacher can post and comment, and students are not allowed.

Other Important Reminders

Remember that the teacher sees all comments and posts of every student. Likewise, the teacher has three options for these comments; Move To Top, Delete or Mute. The Move To Top option will bring the post on top of the Stream page. The Delete button will completely erase the comment, while the Mute option will remove a student's option to post or comment on all posts.

The Stream tab works like Facebook, in that whenever the teacher posts, the post will be on top of the Stream. This is also where all the other comments from the students show up. Users can have a real-time view of the upcoming due dates.

One of the most favorite features of Google Classroom is that it allows teachers to monitor their students during the whole working process. Once the student opens the link to their assignment, the teacher can quickly check on it.

Likewise, the folders that were automatically created once a classroom was created are mainly used for distributing and copying student files. Remember that these folders are not for outside use. If a teacher manually puts a file or a material in the classroom folder, the contents will not be visible to the students, and will not be displayed.

How To Use Google Classroom

The Classroom uses many features of the G Suite such as Google Docs for writing, Gmail for communicating, and Google Calendar for scheduling.

Students are welcomed to their specific classrooms via a private code, developed by the school.

Each class generated would automatically generate a new folder in the Google Drive account of each student, where the students upload their work for the teacher to evaluate.

Teachers can set Google Classroom assignments, arrange due dates in the Google Calendar, and do much more.

How to Create a Class

Classes are fun to create, organize, manage, and remove once they are done. Classes are the most important aspect of this, since it is where everyone will be. If you know how to put all of this together, you will be well on your way to a successful result with Google Classroom.

Now, once you have logged in, it is time to create a class. When you first log in, you will get the option of either student or teacher. Always make sure that you indicate that you are the teacher, and if you mess up, you need to contact the administrator to reset it. It is very important, because students are limited in their options compared to teachers, and it can be quite frustrating. Now, if you are a student, you simply press the (+) button when you get it, to join a class. Teachers need to press on Create A Class.

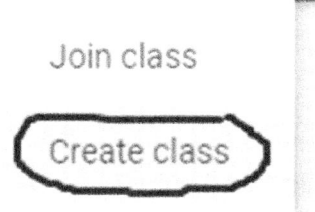

Now, if you have already got classes, chances are you will see some other names there. They will be displayed on the screen itself, but every time you press the (+) button, you will then be able to add more.

Next, you are given a class dialogue boss. You will then type in the name and the section for this. You will be able to create the class immediately from here.

If you want to add more to it, you can go to the About tab, choose the title of the course, along with the description, location and even add materials here. You do need to have a name for the class, since this is how students will find the class when they open it. If you have multiple classes, you will definitely want to specify by either time or day, especially if you have a lot of sections. The Section field is how you do this, and you can create a subject as well, based on the list of subjects they provide for you.

Some teachers like to make these very descriptive, and you should ideally add as much information as you feel that is needed for it. Do remember to not make it some wall of text which will confuse the students. As a teacher, you should make sure students get the information easily, and that they are be able to delineate each class. It is also important to make it easy for your own benefit.

How To Manage A Class

The first thing that you can do when changing the class and managing it, is to give it a theme. One thing you will notice is that you do not have students in there as soon as it is created, so you can have a bit of fun with it. One way to do this is, on the right side, near the header of the general class, you can change the class theme. You can use the themes that are provided. Photos of your class are good options. you can also use different templates for each one, so that you know exactly what theme you are using, because they can sometimes be a bit complicated.

How To Archive, Delete And Copy A Class

Using Google Classroom for teaching purposes may be appropriate, say, at the end of the semester or school period, so that you can archive a class, or delete or restore it, if necessary.

The archived classrooms are moved to an area where you have the materials, student work, and workplaces. You can view them, but you can no longer use them.

Archiving a class is very simple. Choose Class and click on the three-dotted button. You can then select the desired option.

What happens to an archived class? When you

archive a class, it is moved to a separate area to preserve class materials, student work, and posts. You will no longer see it with your active classes on the Classes page. Both teachers and students can view an archived course. To use the class again, you must restore it. Everyone can still access any of the teaching materials in Google Drive, whether they are attachments for homework or other student work. Students cannot unsubscribe from an archived lesson.

An archived class remains in Classroom until it is deleted.

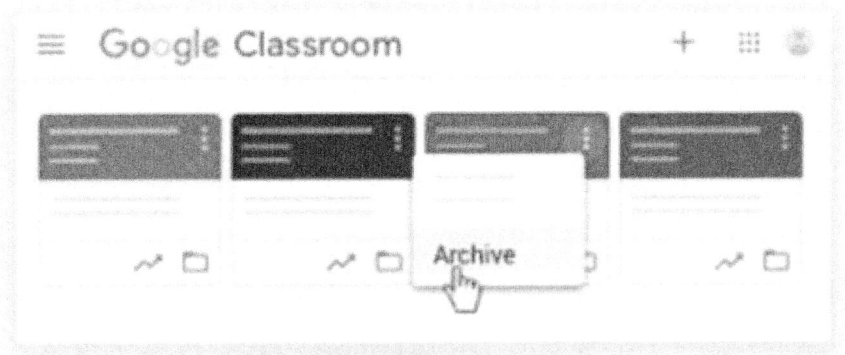

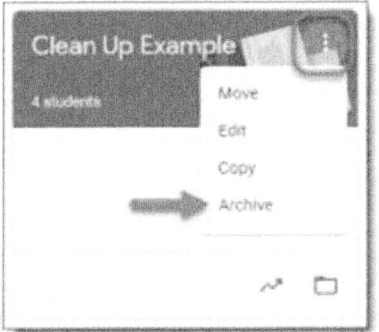

Delete an Archived Class 27

When the teacher decides never to use a class again, he/she can permanently delete it.

You must archive a class before you can delete it. Only the main teacher can delete a class. Co-teachers cannot delete a course.

The teacher will then no longer have access to the class posts or comments. However, teachers and students will still have access to the class files in the class Drive folder.

Warning: It is not possible to cancel the deletion of a class.

Go to Classroom and click Menu at the top.

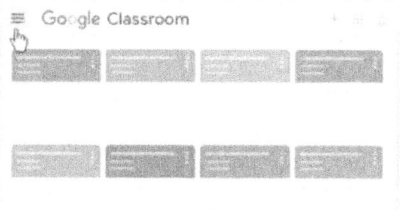

Scroll down, and then click Archived classes

Now click More (three-dotted button), and then Delete and Confirm.

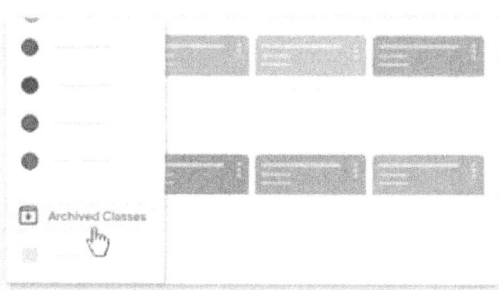

It is also possible to copy a class. This allows you to save time by copying a course you will teach again. In the new class, which retains the original information of the copied class, the teacher's work and grading system will be copied. In contrast, specific elements, such as teacher announcements or student messages, will not be copied. Only teachers and co-teachers can copy a class, and whosoever copies it becomes its primary owner.

Both active classes and archived classes can be copied; the latter when copied become active classes.

To proceed with copying, go to the class you wish to copy. Click More, and then Copy. You can now edit the title and initial information, enter the name of the new class, and click Copy. It should be noted that in the new class, copied homework and questions are saved as drafts.

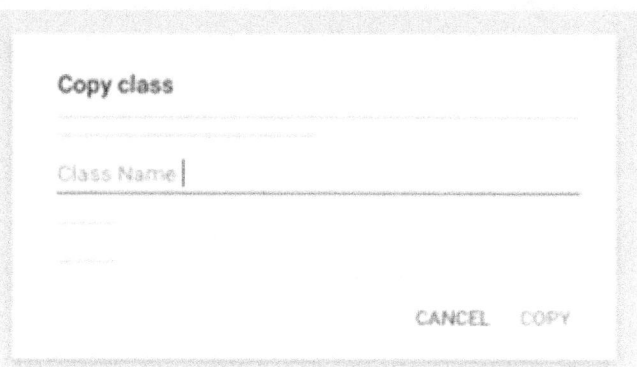

Teachers can manage classes from the Google Classroom homepage by rearranging the class tiles. You can drag and move classes and change the order by dragging the class tile to a new location. This can be done by clicking on the three-dotted button.

Towards the end of the school period, the class can be full of jobs and homework, and it can be difficult to find previous jobs or posts. Teachers can also create new classes during the school year to streamline the workflow.

30

CHAPTER - 3
How to Manage Homework and Assignments

In this section, you will learn how to create an assignment, get it to your students, and then grade it once it is completed. Also, you can learn how to give your students feedback on their work, and how to improve the importance of assignments in the Classroom.

Creating an Assignment

1. The Classroom will always be set to Announcement by default. To get started, click Assignment on your page.

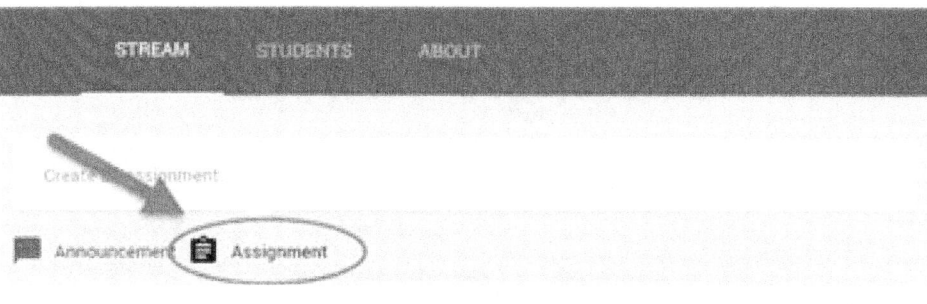

2. Enter the name and description of your task.

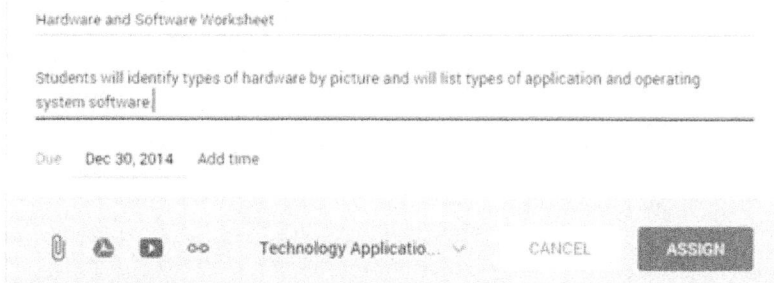

3. Pick the due date (you can change it later). After the assignment is due, the student's Stream will be labeled LATE.

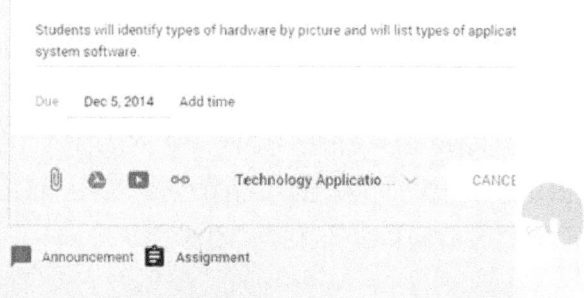

4. Add an optional video/file. You can add a file to your computer, a worksheet from your Google Drive, a photo, or a connection. You should add multiple tools to your task.

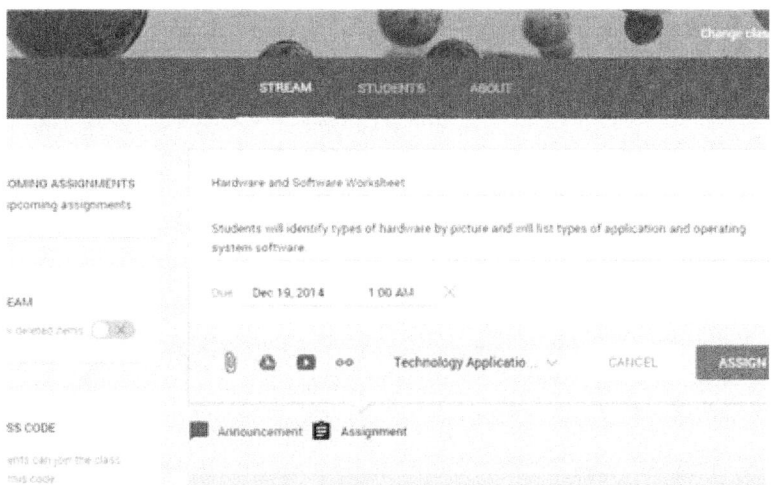

5. Determine if you want students to be able to access the file. Determine whether you want all students to be able to write to the same document, or whether you want each student to receive a specific student name in the file name.

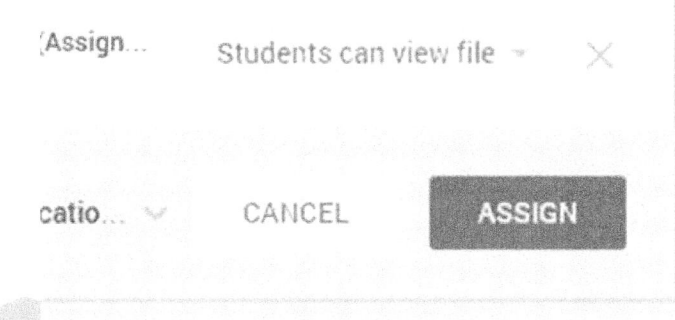

6. Select the parts that you would like to delegate.

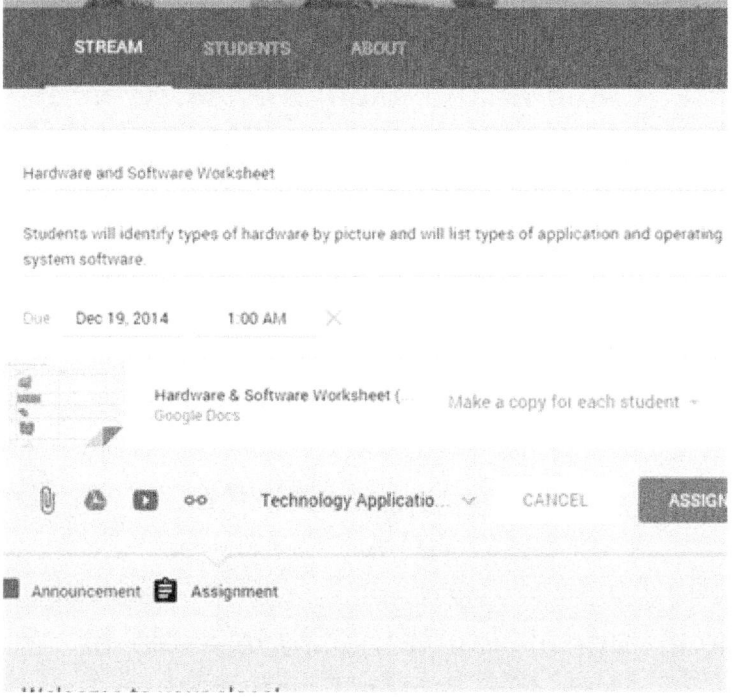

7. Check that all information is right and press ASSIGN.

Editing an Assignment

1. Locate the task on your page, and press three-dotted button in the top-right corner, then select Edit.

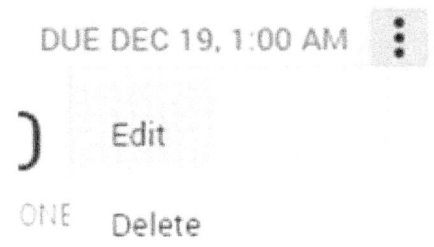

2. You can change:

- Task name
- Definition
- Due date
- Additional resources

You cannot change:

- Task worksheet
- Task grading worksheet

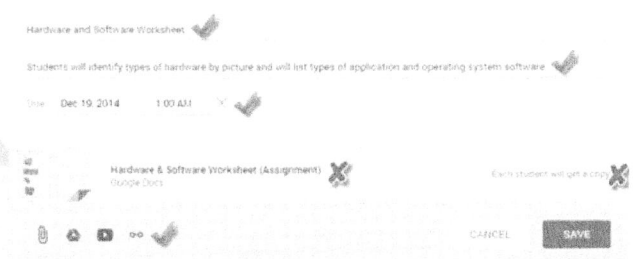

Grading an Assignment

1. Click the title of the assignment you are ready to grade on your Stream.

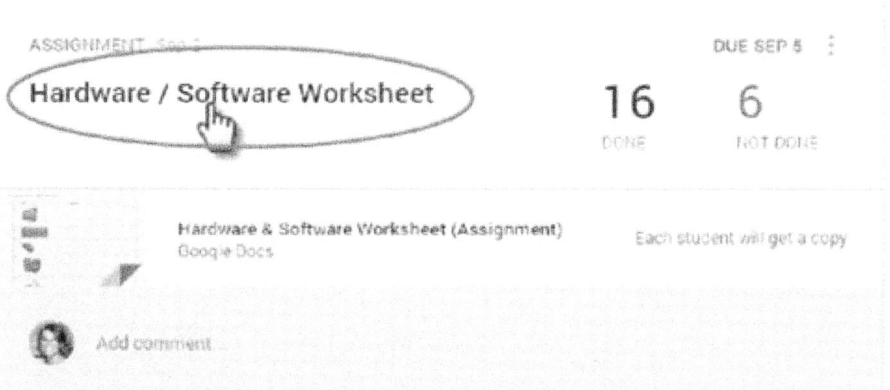

2. OR press the Finished number to see only the students who have completed the task.

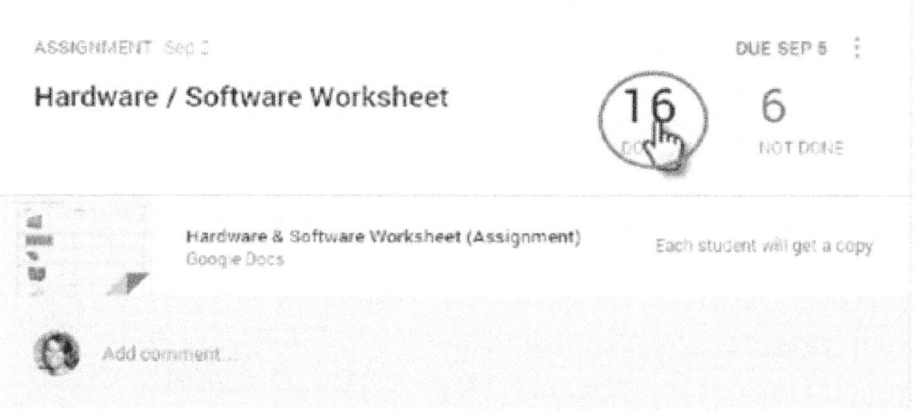

3. Navigate to a student who has not completed his/her task. Tap on the student name, and tap on the worksheet to open and rate it.

4. Use the formatting toolbar to insert comments on the assignment, or to label on it.

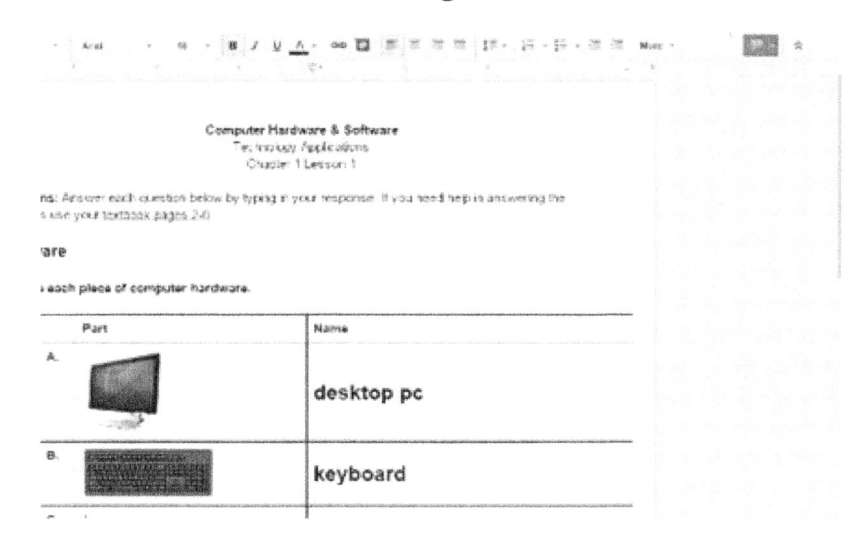

5. The worksheet is opened in a new window. Your comments/markups will be saved automatically. You should close the tab that will take you back to the student assignment list in the Google Classroom. You should input the grade for the student right now.

RETURNED	8/10
LATE	No Grade
RETURNED	9/10

6. Scroll to the top and press RETURN to give the file back to the student.

Sending Feedback To Students

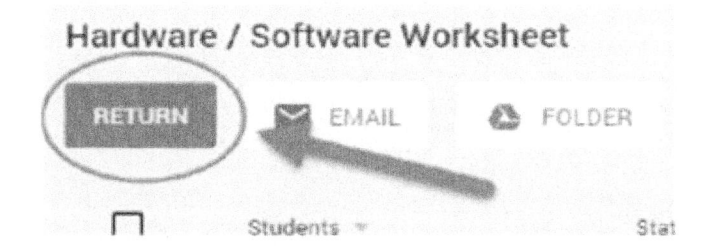

1. Choose the assignment that you want to leave any suggestions or remarks on. Find and click on the student's name.

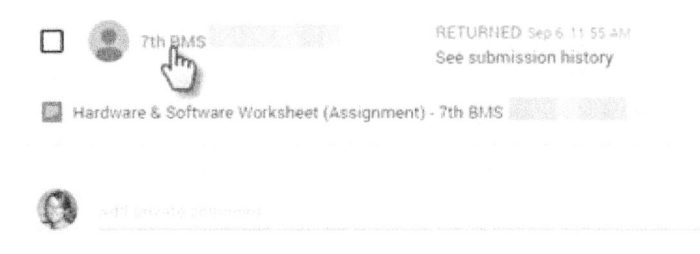

2. Where it says Private comments, write a message to the student and then click POST.

3. The student will be able to respond to the explanations you have given.

Changing Points is Possible

1. Open the assignment you want to the set points for. Locate the Points box in the top-right corner.

2. You can either click the drop-down arrow next to the point value and pick the number, or you can click on 10 and enter the value you want to assign.

Click Fix when asked if you are sure you want to update the value of the amount.

Downloading Student Grades

1. Open the assignment for which you would like to access the score. Find the DOWNLOAD button at the top of the list.

2. Click the button to either access This assignment or All assignments.

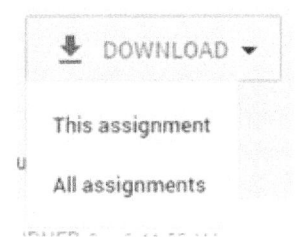

3. Select the location of the file, name of the file, and then press Delete.

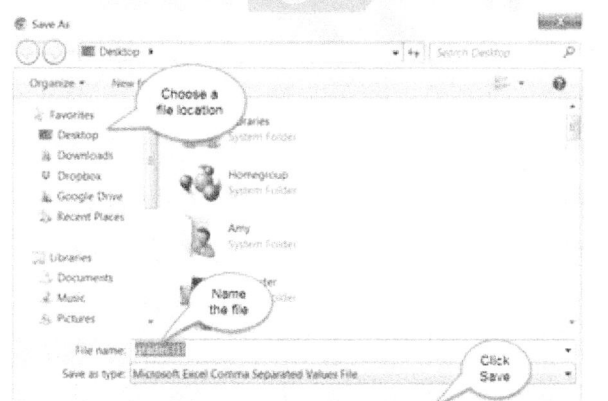

4. Find the file on your computer and open it to see the ratings on the spreadsheet.

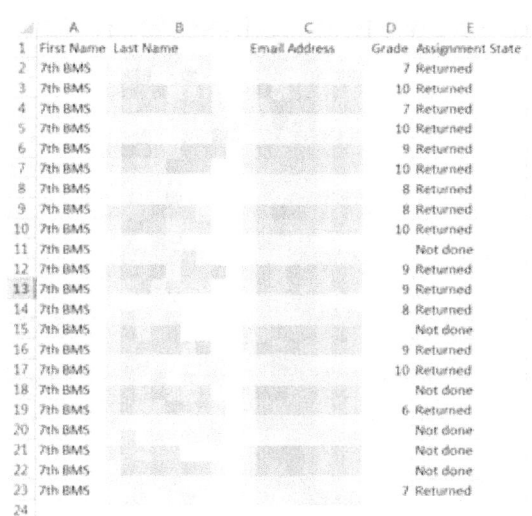

GOOGLE CLASSROOM

GOOGLE CLASSROOM

CHAPTER - 4
Managing Classes for Students

Student View: A Quick Tour

Stream: The Stream is where students can view Google Classroom assignments and announcements posted.

Classmates: Students can view a list of the other students enrolled in the Google Classroom in the Classmates tab.

About: The About tab contains details about the class that the instructor uploaded. Tools, such as the syllabus and other class-related documents that are not assignments, can be located for conveniently on the About page.

Share with Your Class: The students can post a global comment or question to the class, at the top of the page. Students may include files, links, or Google Drive documents in their comments to the Stream. However, teachers may mute the student to prevent them from doing this from the Students tab.

Assignments: The left-hand side of the screen shows a pane with a list of assignments due soon. You can also access the full list of assignments by clicking on View All in the assignment pane. This list is located in the upper-left corner, through the Menu icon.

Menu: Students can switch classes, go back to the main menu, or display a list of their assignments via the upper-left-corner Menu icon.

Announcements: Reports posted as announcements by the teacher are produced for students as View Only. Students can read them, and open any attached files or links in the advertisement.

Add Comment: Students may post a reply or question to any announcement or assignment, unless the teacher has muted them. Students cannot attach files or links to notices or assignments.

Assignment: Students can find assignments posted by the instructor in the Stream, and then access links or attachments directly from the Stream in the assignment. Documents given by the teacher's assignment template are not visible in Stream. Templates are displayed on the submission screen for the task.

Open: A Close button is available for every task. Students press the Close button to reveal the application screen for the task.

Assignment Submission Screen

Google Classroom lets students upload their digital work. Clicking on the Open button from the assignment will take students to the Submission page for assignments. If the instructor has decided to include a template for part of the assignment, the template documents given to the students will be available. Students should add additional files, and use the Submission page for assignments to hand in their work.

Google Classroom has a free Download in the Application Store option for both Android and iOS devices. The application lets students view and upload their work in the class Stream. Even when offline, the students can access the Stream in the application. The Google Classroom software also allows students to use the application to take pictures of their work, and upload the photographs as an assignment.

The Google Classroom software allows sharing of Google Files, Google Slides and Google Sheets from other applications. Work done with these different

GOOGLE CLASSROOM

applications can be sent from the other application to Google Classroom. This helps students to share their ideas using a variety of applications/devices.

Join a Class

To join a class using class codes, students log on to their Classroom account and select the Add Class icon. Then they select Join Class to enter the code in the provided field. After submitting, the student immediately becomes a member of the class. After the class is filled with students, the teacher disables the code to prevent its abuse. The system can be switched back on at will, when the need arises.

Students using an email address different from the school's domain require special permission from the school G Suite administrator, to allow external domain accounts to join classes.

Un-enroll From A Class

You can no longer see the class in the Classroom when you unenrolled from it, but all your class files will be saved in your Google Drive.

If you have mistakenly unregistered from a class and need to re-register, see Enter a class as a student.

Note: From Android iPhone & iPad devices, you cannot unregister from an existing class. Contact your instructor, and ask them to unarchive the class to unregister.

1. Go to classroom.google.com.
2. Select the Classes tab.
3. Press Unenrolled for more on the lesson.
4. Press Unenrolled to confirm.

View An Archived Class

Your teacher could archive it once a class ends. Archiving a class, extracts it from your Classroom homepage and positions it in a separate area, which makes it easier to manage your website.

Even teachers can record a lesson or delete it. If you want to delete a class from your homepage, Unenrollment from a class is needed.

Note: You are not allowed to unregister from an archived class.

When Archiving A Class

1. It is deleted from your homepage.
2. You can see associated materials, but you cannot upload any work.
3. Google Drive class folder also helps you to access

class materials.

4. You cannot unsubscribe from this. Ask your instructor to do so, if you need to unenroll from an archived class.

Android iPhone & iPad Computers

1. Go to classroom.google.com.

2. Click Menu at the end.

3. Tap Archived Classes and scroll down.

4. Tap on the class you wish to see.

Note: If you have not saved any of your courses, this option does not appear on the menu.

View Your Class Resource Page

Teachers in Classroom can have video meetings. All video meetings produced in Classroom are called nicknamed meetings, because if the teacher is the last person to quit, students cannot start or enter the meeting a meeting before the teacher. Such permissions will vary according to how the school administrator sets up Google Meet.

Meet in the Classroom

1. Teachers and students use school accounts and are on the same domain.

2. Admins are expected to turn Google Meet on.

3. Admins will find more help for distance learning at Setting up Meet.

See The Current Work On The Stream Page

The latest research and updates can be seen on the Stream tab. The new post is still up at the top.

1. Go to classroom.google.com.

2. Click on the link.

3. Click on the task of the query to see any guidance or feedback (optional).

See The Work Grouped By Subject On The Classwork Page

Your instructor can organize work by subjects on the Classwork page, such as homework or essays.

1. Go to classroom.google.com.

2. Click on the link.

3. Click on Classwork, at the end.

4. Look for a question or assignment under a subject.

5. To show any directions or suggestions, click on Assignment show or Question view link (optional).

Check For Late Or Missed Assignments

The instructor establishes the late work policies for the class. The classroom is not stopping you from handing in late work, however.

When assigning work to your instructor, it is labeled Assigned. Depending on whether you hand in your work on time, Late or Completed would be reported. For example, when a project is due at 9:00 AM, hand it in at 8:59 AM. It is late when you hand it in at 9:00 AM.

1. Go to classroom.google.com.
2. Click Your work on a class file.
3. To the right, you see the work status of each item, which can be one of the following:

- Assigned — job assigned by your instructor. See your due date.
- Turned in — work that came in on time.
- Graded — you see your score for graduated research that your instructor has returned.
- Returned — you see a check for ungraded work returned by your instructor.
- Missing — you did not sign up to work.

- Hand in—done late/work you did late.

4. Click on the element for more details; to extend it, click Details view (optional).

For more ways to see your work status and monitor your work, go to see for a class at your work.

Connecting with Your Classmates

Post To The Class Stream

If your teacher allows, you can use posts, comments, and replies to communicate with your class on the Stream page.

1. A post is a piece of knowledge or query that you add to a Stream of the class. (For example: "When are we going to visit the museum?")

2. A comment is a response to a message or a comment. (For instance: "We're going next Friday.")

3. An answer is an answer to a statement by someone who discusses them. (For example: "Thanks to (name + commenter)!")

Not all teachers on the Stream page allow updates and comments.

Note: You can submit a private message to your teacher about an assignment or question, if you do not want to add to the Stream list.

Create A Post

To ask a question or exchange details with your teacher and classmates, build a message.

1. Go to classroom.google.com.
2. Click on the link.
3. Click on Share with your class on the Stream tab.

   Note: If you cannot see Share with your class, your instructor has not given post permissions.

4. Enter what you want to say, and then press Mail.

Use & Mention, To Share Messages

If you want to capture somebody's attention when you submit a post in the Classroom, use (+) or (@) with the person's email address to mention them. You may include classmates or your instructor, or both, in class Stream comments or answers, to either invite them to enter a discussion or to show your post.

For example, you can send your answer when your teacher posts a question, and also mention a classmate, for him to enter the discussion with your teacher.

When you use (+) or (@) to name someone in your comment or reply, the person you listed will receive an email, if they have alerts set up in their account settings.

Note mentions (+) or (@) only function in the class line.

To address someone:

1. Go to classroom.google.com.
2. Click on the link.
3. Write a message in the comment box Add Class, or in the class box Post if you are making a new post.
4. Enter (+) or (@). An Auto-Complete list of classmates appears when you type the person's name.
5. Press Enter to pick the first name, and add the email address to the box.
6. Scroll down the list to pick a name, and press Enter to pick a specific name.
7. Click the Mail icon.

Note: If the name you want is not shown in the Auto-Complete list, enter the full email address

Send An Email

In the Classroom, you can contact your teachers and classmates.

1. Use your school account to provide an email. This account is also known as a training account for the G Suite. See About Classroom User Accounts to learn about your account.

2. The school administrator will turn on the email. In the Classroom, on the People page, the administrator has turned off an email if you do not see Email next to a name.

Share to Classroom From A Mobile Device

You can attach webpages from your mobile device to new tasks, questions, or updates in a class, without having to leave the page that you share. You can build a new assignment without going to the Classroom first, if you see the Share to Classroom button on a web page. Like other social media icons on the website, you can consider Link to Classroom.

1. Tap More Share Classroom on the website, connect, photo, or picture.

2. The latter active class is selected by default. Tap Next to pick another class to modify the class.

3. Select the relevant option for the post you would like to use.

4. Tap Post. Complete the task, issue, or announcement.

GOOGLE CLASSROOM

CHAPTER - 5
Google Docs and Google Sheets

What is Google Docs?

If you have always looked for the best way to introduce technology into your Classroom, to improve the interaction between you and your students and get quick feedback, then Google Docs is for you.

Google Docs is am effective online word processing software that allows you to save all your documents and files on Google Drive freely. The basic requirement is an active Google account (Gmail).

When you use Google Docs, your files are automatically stored on Google Cloud, and you can access them anywhere you go, provided you are connected to the internet.

Files created on Google Docs can be shared, and you can decide to share them with others and control how they interact with the files. Say you went on an adventure with some friends and wrote a detailed article about the trip, but you did not want your friend to alter the content of the article. On Google Docs, you can give them 'read-only' permission.

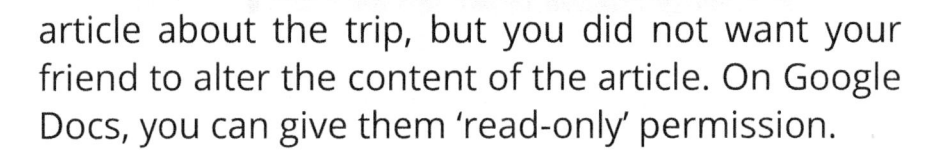

Without making a single purchase or installing any application, everyone can enjoy using Google Docs. This makes it an excellent tool for your classroom. But how do you introduce it to your students? Here are some ways of doing that.

Introducing Google Docs to Students

An effective collaborative method, using Google Docs in your classroom will yield excellent results. There are several unique features of this application that would inspire all of us.

Collaborative Writing and Editing

Having divided the class into groups and provided each group with an assignment of reviewing books or writing a paper, it might be the students in the group to come together and work on the assignment, as their ideas will likely all be different.

As such, the collaborative feature of Google Docs will make the task easier. They will be able to work together as a team. Each one can contribute to the assignment, by working on the same document others are working on, but without seeing others.

Changes will be seen by other students in the classroom or group, and can be reviewed immediately. As such, everyone can enjoy working on the same document, and complete their tasks efficiently without seeing each other.

Google Docs comes with referencing tools that will help student with references. The Smart Spell Checker will also ensure that there are no spelling errors in the assignment submitted, and that everything comes out well.

The research tool provides students with further opportunities to engage in real-world writing, and they can insert links easily, while also enjoying easy citation using the handy one-click feature.

Google Docs also provides support for students who make use of other sources for their writing. For one, it integrates with EasyBib and other popular tools.

Translation

The ability of Google Docs to translate files from English to other languages like French, Spanish, Dutch, etc. makes it even more useful. Amazingly, this is an easy thing to do; all that is expected is to click Tool, select Translate Document, select the language for the translation, and sit back while your document is translated accurately for you.

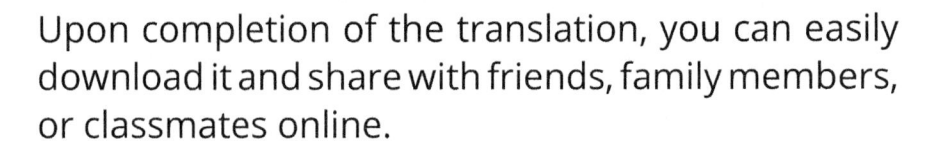

Upon completion of the translation, you can easily download it and share with friends, family members, or classmates online.

For Collaborative Brainstorming

When students brainstorm together, they improve their chances of developing ideas and reaching their goals quickly.

Google Docs makes this easier. Every digital brainstorming session will help the students offer their ideas, to reach the common goal of solving the problem at hand.

The presence of tools like shapes, arrows, text, and the ability to import images to build a visual map for the task makes brainstorming easier. You can review what each student is doing, as each adjustment they make comes with a different color in Google Docs. This makes tracking progress easier. Overall, everyone will be able to contribute to the success of the assignment.

Quick Self-Grading Quiz

You can easily deliver feedback and increase your students' motivation by creating a self-grading quiz through Google Forms.

Create a simple quiz featuring multiple-choice questions. Take the quiz to supply the correct answers. Adding a little formula into your spreadsheet will make it easier for the grading to be automated.

When everyone submits, you can publish their results immediately and help your students understand how to use the Find tool (Ctrl + F) to search for their score. You should endeavor to protect the privacy of your students, by asking them to sign in with a unique identifier.

Virtual Copy Machine

You can easily provide a starting point for your student's digital projects via the use of a Google Docs template. You can make use of the consistent page format and template features, to create your own unique format.

Google Docs works like a virtual copy machine, as it comes with numerous user-submitted templates that are already created and available for everyone. There is a special category designed for students and teachers. You will definitely enjoy this tool.

Conclusively, the functions and features of Google Docs are currently changing. As such, more improvements are still expected. It is likely that soon, it will become the best option for teaching and learning. It is time you try it out and see the wonder it delivers.

Introducing Google Sheets in Your Classroom

Google's G Suite is a tested and efficient platform that is great for schools, teachers, and students when it comes to one-on-one classroom communication. Google Sheets is one of the tools provided in the G Suite platform.

Many view it as a data collection and organization tool. It is a flexible tool that makes data collection, resource management, inventory management, and documentation easier.

Digital Portfolios with Google Forms

The expert combination of Google Forms and Google Sheets leads to an improvement in the individual use of the tools as a simple digital portfolio tool. Google Forms also allows responders to upload a file within the form, in response to the original form sent.

In the image above, the process is carefully outlined. It shows a student creating a form as an entry tool for archiving elements and artifacts for a digital portfolio. The options are numerous as students can upload files like images, documents, videos, audio files, etc.

Upon collecting the response on the spreadsheet, the digital portfolio belonging to the student can then be shared with the teacher for review purposes, and the teacher can also add feedback.

It is essential to note that all the files uploaded with the form are automatically saved on your Google Drive. To enable the teacher to open and view the files, it is important to ensure that the files are shared with the teacher. The teacher could also add entries to the student form, to assist them in archiving the portfolio.

A teacher can also create their form with a drop-down menu question, which will contain students' names. The teacher will be able to archive the student's work in a spreadsheet, which can then be easily sorted while checking the work.

Digital Rubrics and Rubric Portfolios

Another benefit of rethinking Google Sheets is that it improves the overall process of creating, using, and sharing rubrics in the classroom, for students using G Suite. There are several advantages to rubrics on Google Sheets compared to using rubrics that are paper-based.

For one, Google Sheets-based master rubrics can be duplicated and used for future assignments. Additionally, within a sheet with a master rubric, one can easily duplicate the master rubrics within the sheet for easy assessment of submitted tasks. As such, the teacher can have one sheet for each assignment he/she accesses with the master rubric.

In every sheet, teachers can create tabs for each student. This will make it easier for the teacher to document the rubrics, and organize them in a spreadsheet for every assignment given.

Since the rubrics are in digital format, the teacher can make use of conditional formatting and formulas. With conditional formatting, the teacher can incorporate rules on sheet rubrics, which can affect the text and cell color.

For example, a rule might state that for every period (.) in a cell, the cell automatically changes to a blue color, and the text becomes slanted. The addition of a period to each cell will make color-coding of the rubrics instant and effective.

The addition of a formula in the sheet rubrics will make score calculation easier. These will be recorded instantly in a scoring column. The addition of the formula and the conditional formatting will result in adding a period (.) in a cell, to create the coded text and box, to deliver automatic grading.

Class Resources Sheet

Google Classroom is an effective tool. Undoubtedly, it is a tool that can help manage digital workflow in a one-to-one G Suite classroom environment. However, there are other options you have for sharing and posting resources and assignments in the Classroom, through Google Sheets.

The process of using the Sheet consists of the teacher redesigning a sheet to mirror a course calendar, that will contain columns labelled 'Date,' 'Time,' 'Chapter,' 'Unit,' etc.

The teacher can also include columns for assignments, slides, notes, video playlists, and homework, among others. The good thing is that a teacher can skillfully organize a complete course into a unique sheet.

You can continue to add more sheets as your class progresses. You can add them as tabs across the bottom, and use them to differentiate between quarters, units of study, or semesters. By simply creating a course folder on Google Drive, a teacher can easily share and make the course content available for all students. By giving them the link, anyone can view these documents.

As such, all students can open the course material and copy it for further reading when they have 'read-only' access. You can also use this approach with Google Classroom. On the About page of the classroom, you can put the course sheet as a permanent resource.

When it is time to collect all assignments, students can easily duplicate the original template file from their sheet, and submit their assignment via Google Classroom. With this feature, there will be a significant drop in the number of posts the teacher will make in the Classroom during a course.

Research Planning & Archiving

It can be very stressful and challenging for teachers to prepare their students for detailed research. However, with Google Sheets, teachers can give their students a well-structured approach, which will make it easier for them to organize, categorize, and track the entire research process.

It will be easier for students to track their progress by creating headings in their sheets. Examples of headings may include 'Source,' 'Original Text,' 'Summary,' 'Conclusion,' etc. This will make the identification of the crucial elements present in the task easier, and will help them understand the concept better.

Upon completion of the research process, and when the student starts to convert their research into papers, they can then use these subheadings, keyword columns, and other essential filters in the sheet to limit the view of their research. If they need to search for keywords, they can make use of the Find on page function in their browser.

GOOGLE CLASSROOM

CHAPTER - 6
Introducing Google Slides in Your Classroom

If you have been using Microsoft PowerPoint, you will have a clearer idea of what Google Slides is. MS PowerPoint is often used for creating presentation slides.

Google Slides is closely related to PowerPoint, but unlike PowerPoint, it is hosted online and allows many people to collaborate and work on the same presentation at the same time. Here are some quick facts about Google Slides:

- Google Slides is free.
- There is a blank document you can start your presentation from, or you can make use of pre-designed templates.
- You can access it via the web on all internet-enabled devices like PC, Android, iOS, etc., and also via a desktop application on Google Chrome OS.

- You can easily import PowerPoint files into Google Slides, and then edit them. Slides can be exported as PowerPoint files, PDF, JPEG, or PNG files.

- You can add images, audio, and video to presentations.

- The sharing options for Google Slides are numerous. You can make it private, or you can select a few people to share it with. You can even make it available for the wider public. You can also choose if people can only view it, or view and edit the presentation.

- When collaborating with others on Google Slides, you can chat with them, leave comments, and work together on the slides at the same time.

- Saving your work as your presentation is automatic.

- You can first present your slide within the Slides (View > Present). You can also either connect your system to a screen, or make use of AirPlay or Chromecast in showcasing the presentation to a live audience.

- The presentation can also be done live on Google Hangout.

- You can quickly add captions to your work while presenting on Google Slides.

- Google Slides comes with numerous add-ons. These third-party tools enable you to get more functions on your Google Slides. Most of them are free, while some are premium versions.

You can embed Google Slides in blogs and websites.

How to Prepare a Google Slide Presentation

If you try the method provided above for starting a Google Slide presentation, you will have the option to either build a blank presentation or use a pre-designed template. Irrespective of the options, everyone can conveniently and easily create a presentation.

Below are some essentials that will help you create an excellent Google Slides presentation.

- Include text through text boxes (you can drag and drop them wherever you like).

- Insert important elements using the Insert function on the main toolbar. You can insert elements like images, videos, audios, shapes, charts, tables, word art, diagrams, or animations.

- With the (+) button, add new slides.

- Duplicating slides can be done by right-clicking on the navigation panel to the left. This is easier than building slides from scratch. The duplicate function is also present under the Slide menu.

How to Use Google Slides in the Classroom

When you create a slide deck, using Google Slides becomes easier. This is the combination of several slides for the creation of a single presentation. Many use a slide deck for supporting oral presentations.

Here are some situations where teachers or students might need to make use of the basic slide deck:

- Slides can be created when you wish to support the lessons presented to your students.
- If students are planning an oral presentation, they can prepare slides as part of their homework.
- Both students and teachers can also create slide decks when they need to showcase learning, or when sharing school programs is needed in, say, a school assembly, information evening, etc.
- Collaboration on the slide deck may be required for conferences and staff meeting presentations.

These are some of the things you can do with Google Slides, and they are just some of the basics.

More About Google Slides

As an effective presentation product, which is very similar to the popular PowerPoint, Google Slides is needed in your classroom.

Since it is part of the Google Suite product, it is free to use. Below are six ways you can make use of Google Slides in your classroom.

1. Presentation Becomes Simplified

When giving a lecture or presentation with Google Slides, you can easily add visual content, which will help make your point clearer. According to research, it has been noticed that using visual representation will help your student remember what they are taught via visuals than audio. This is because they can see the information.

2. It Improves Student Participation

With the use of practical EdTech tools like Pear Deck and Poll Everywhere, you can easily request feedback inside Google Slides. They are effective tools that can be used for formative assessment and also can be used for improving the engagement of students in the classroom.

3. Collaborative Learning Is Improved

With Google Slides, teachers can improve collaborative learning. You can design assignments in such a way that every student will create their own slides, and they can eventually combine them into a single presentation that they can all learn from.

Alternatively, you can create small groups and ask them to work on presenting a slide in real-time for the whole class. This improves students' engagement in the presentation.

4. Flipping The Classroom Is Easier

With Google Slides, teachers can skillfully flip the classroom. The popular method of learning is to accept new information from school and practice them on your own at home. With Google Slides, this model is improved.

Students can make use of presentation slides created by teachers for their personal learning at home, but before they leave the class, they can also practice with the slides.

One unique and excellent thing about Google Slides is that you can easily integrate it with other Google products like Sheets or Charts.

5. An Excellent Alternative For Notecards

For easy brainstorming, organization, and researching of their projects, students can make use of Google Slides. Google Slides can be used as digital notecards that can be used for memorizing vocabulary or other materials.

It can be explored as a journal or log, and can be used as a tracker to track the performance of your students. You can also use it for personal items, like as a diary or personal records.

6. Used As An Effective Drawing Program

Google Slides can be used effectively as a drawing program. As such, students can draw on their slides, and they can also paint on them or make shapes. They can also create comic strips on slides.

76

CHAPTER - 7
Hidden Google Classroom Features

While Google Classroom gives numerous incredible benefits, there are three that can specifically spare instructors and students a lot of time and further increment work process effectiveness. Along these lines, we should exploit these exciting highlights!

The Assignment Calendar

Google Classroom makes an Assignment Calendar to help keep students and educators composed. Each time an educator makes a task or question within Google Classroom, and connects a due date to it, the task shows on the class schedule within Google Classroom right away.

Educators will, likewise, see that another Calendar currently shows up in their G Suite Calendar. Not exclusively, teachers are able to add assignments to this schedule through Classroom. They can likewise directly get to it by means of G Suite Calendar, to include occasions for the class that may not be attached to a due date. A few instances of instructors utilizing this schedule work include booking class field trips, setting up additional mentoring time, and composing an after-school meeting. To make the schedule progressively available, consider making it open in the Calendar settings, and sharing the URL interface with guardians.

The Work Area

Educators and students can likewise exploit the Work region within Google Classroom to accumulate every exceptional task into one area. On the off chance that an instructor has not evaluated a specific task, it will show here. Thus, if a student has not turned in a task, it will likewise show in their Work region. In this way, the Work territory acts as a de facto task list, and can support educators. Students distinguish and deal with their work process adequately.

Organize the class Stream with Topics

Subjects, another component within Google Classroom, permits educators to sort out the presents that they add on the Classroom Stream. When making a declaration, task, or question, instructors would now be able to dole out a point, and these points go about as a classification for each post, which permits them to be composed proficiently.

When another subject is made, it will show on the left half of the Classroom Stream, and when a theme is chosen, all posts that have been doled out that point will show up. The Topics highlight currently permits instructors to sort out the entirety of the substance within their course. For instance, a history instructor may make a point for every unit of study, say for example 'Old Rome.' A math educator may decide to make a theme for every unit or part that they study.

Share to Classroom Extension

For educators utilizing Chromebooks or workstations in their classrooms, the Share to Classroom Chrome Extension permits instructors to show and offer student work and screens effectively, with the class. By utilizing the Share to Classroom extension, students can share a website to their instructor's PC. In the first place, students click the extension, then they select Push to Teacher. When done, the educator gets a pop-up warning on his/her screen, saying he/she should acknowledge before the student's page is shown.

By following similar advances, an educator can

push out a website to their students' gadgets continuously!

The extension likewise permits educators to make Google Classroom content right from the augmentation. In the event that an instructor finds a website he might want to post in Google Classroom as a feature of a task, question, or declaration, he can make any of those alternatives by using the augmentation.

By utilizing the Share to Classroom extension, instructors and students are ready to share new disclosures and stories, effectively and successfully.

CHAPTER - 8
How Google Docs Can Help You Work with Student

Google Docs is an easy-to-understand set-up of online community-oriented instruments that have a massive potential use in the classroom. A year ago, the entirety of the students in our school got Google Docs records. I was kept occupied with getting students and teachers fully operational with the new tools, then finding inventive approaches to utilize them as compelling instruments for learning. Here are some of the top choices.

Community-oriented Writing

Sharing and remarking furnish students with chances to get prompt criticism on their composition from teachers and companions in the everyday classroom. The incorporated Reference tool and Special Spell Checker give students help in on the page. The inherent research device extends open doors for students to take part in genuine composition, and smooths out the way toward making connections and references with a single, helpful tick. For students utilizing an assortment of sources in their composition, Google Docs incorporates consistently with EasyBib.

Google Docs Writing Workshop Inbox

One of the difficulties of utilizing Google Docs in a class loaded with students is in dealing with every one of those Google Docs. While it is genuinely simple for students to learn to share their work with teachers, the mess that winds up in teacher's email boxes can be overwhelming. To take care of this issue, John Miller thought of utilizing a Google Form to gather assignments. Here is how John's development works:

- Teachers make and distribute a Google Form to be utilized as an Inbox.

- When it is an ideal opportunity to turn in a Google Docs, students total the straightforward shape, and present a connect to their Google Docs.

- The data presented by students naturally populates a spreadsheet to be utilized by teachers to monitor assignments, and to rapidly get to those assignments for evaluating and audit.

Utilize a Google Form as an Inbox

Self-grading Quiz

Furnish students with prompt input and increment inspiration, by making a straightforward self-evaluating test with a Google Form. Simply make a test with a couple of numerous decision questions. Take the test yourself to present the right answers, and pop a straightforward equation into the spreadsheet end to let the technology do the reviewing for you. Promptly distribute the spreadsheet of results, and teach students how to utilize the Discover tool (Control + F) to rapidly discover their score, and significantly up the ante to build student inspiration. If it is not too much trouble, stay away from open mortification and hard sentiments; ensure you expect students to sign in with a type of special identifier that secures their protection.

Utilize A Google Form to Make A Self-evaluating Test

A Virtual Copy Machine

If you are searching for a simple and proficient approach to furnish students with a beginning stage for an advanced undertaking, Google Docs Templates can help. You can spare time and guide the learning, by furnishing students with a reliable page position, and utilizing and making your own layouts. A Google Docs layout resembles a virtual copier. There are a lot of client-submitted formats previously made, and accessible for open use and there is even a class for students and teachers.

By consolidating different sorts of technology in your classroom, you can spare time for yourself and your students, and you can make a superior correspondence framework between students, teachers, and guardians. Powerful correspondence is a key segment of a fruitful class.

Co-ordinated Effort Is A Breeze

There are numerous methods for teaming up in Google applications, so regardless of what the task is, Google can help. By utilizing Drive and Docs, students can chip away at similar papers together, whenever they want. With highlights like remarks and proposals, it is astounding how we, at any point, achieved anything great by composing our own segments at home and assembling them in class.

Another incredible path for students to team up with each other is with Hangouts. Video conferencing is an extremely helpful approach to hold a speedy (or long) meeting from the solace of home, or when in a hurry! Gathering work can be a significant learning technique, and we need to make it as simple as conceivable, to get students concentrated on the task rather than dealing with communication issues.

Parent-Teacher Communication Is Very Easy

Talking about gatherings, Hangouts is ideal for occupied guardians. They can send a speedy message to you to plan a video gathering, and you can meet with them (on the web, obviously!) whenever it is convenient for both of you. On the other hand, you can keep a Google Calendar for guardians, to plan their meetings that way—there are many potential outcomes. Keeping guardians educated is a significant advancement to student achievement, and these are some extremely simple approaches to do that.

Everybody Is Familiar with Google

Basically, everybody has utilized an application/service made by Google. I cannot explain how tremendous Google is—the company either owns or makes a huge amount of the online assets that we use. Who has not utilized Google Search, Images, Maps, or YouTube? Google makes their products/services for everybody to utilize, so they are both easy to utilize and limitlessly compatible with most gadgets. It just bodes well to utilize something that everybody can comprehend.

CHAPTER - 9
Google Classroom: An Interactive Platform

Engagement Through Videos

Educators can provide grades or reviews electronically without ever having to deal with paperwork by using open technology. Additionally, all work on the course is saved, so that students can revisit it while they are at home. Students can also complete assignments via Google Classroom and communicate with teachers. This two-way communication method makes teaching and learning using the platform more convenient. By incorporating video, it makes engaging students even more comfortable.

Below are some reasons why videos could be helpful in a Google Classroom:

- Video facilitates collaboration and learning: In Google Classroom, multimedia is used by educators to improve the coursework. Many are making videos within their class as interactive learning resources. By using video platforms, educators can create video tutorials or lessons, provide student input, use as assignments for students, or capture lectures all with a click of the record button.

- Feasibility in access: By using videos, educators can interact effectively, and keep students learning without ever having to waste time in class. The videos are sent home and viewed in flipped or blended learning scenarios. The student will learn from home, which makes them more interested in the Classroom.

The Classroom is an online application that can be used anywhere. Educators are given access to their videos on multiple devices with an account. They can quickly jump between devices and have access to video recordings.

With the Chromebook applications, educators and students both can record and share their videos. Videos can be stored directly on Google Drive. All files uploaded are stored in a folder in the Classroom. This makes videos easily accessible to teachers as well as students.

- Saves Time: Video is incredible for timesaving. Forget about typing out long assignments or grading documents! With video, educators can film assignments and be able to assign them all in a few minutes. The educators will add a video file with instructions when they make an assignment in a Classroom.

- Encourages teamwork and communication: Video encourages collaboration and strengthens conversations. Google Classroom gives students several ways to work together. Teachers can encourage online student-to-student discussions and create group projects within the tool. Students will hold talks with each other using video, and complete tasks as assigned to them. Also, students can collaborate on Google Docs and share their work with teachers easily.

It is an immersive, learning environment that is collaborative. By using videos, they can further enrich the experience. With Classroom, teachers can separate assignments, integrate videos and web pages into classes, and create shared group assignments for students.

- Strengthens the student-teacher bond: Videos provide a more reliable link with the students. Positive feedback is needed for students to learn. This is a worthy aspect of all learning. So why not do it by video? Recent studies have shown that at a higher level, video mentoring and feedback requires students to communicate with teachers. It gives them a bond that they would otherwise not get in a group environment. Video offers a one-to-one friendship without being face-to-face.

Google Classroom educators can easily grade assignments. They can give any student personalized feedback. There is also the opportunity to comment on the grading tool. Additionally, the Classroom application in smartphones helps users to annotate research. Google Classroom can save all kinds of grades quickly.

Record the video, go to the screen recorder and press the Record button. You need to upload and publish the video when it is finished, and provide the students with the link. They can access it from anywhere.

Film and share every instructional video with your students. You can monitor them while they watch the video lecture. You will be able to see if your pupils watched your video. You will also realize when the students started watching exactly, and what section they kept reverting to. Video analytics help you understand what interests or engages your students, which part of the video needs further detail, and where your students lose interest.

Engagement Through Student-Student Interaction

Initially, while using the Class Comment feature, teachers did find some sorts of distractions-there was all the usual chatter, typical of social media. However, once the students started using Google Classroom, the teachers began to note a slightly unexpected advantage of the Class Comment feature: students began to answer each other's questions. In their online Google classrooms, not all classes or students do this, but the ones who do, excel. While teachers need to step in and answer a few questions, students do teach one another for the most part!

The Student Response System (SRS) built into the platform is a prominent new feature. This helps teachers to inject questions into the Stream page of the Classroom, and start question-driven discussions with students answering each other's questions. Teachers may post a video, photo, or article, for example, and include a question that they want their students to answer. This way, teachers can learn and check in on the progress of their students, which is a fundamental practice. They can do that very quickly with this new functionality, from anywhere, at any moment.

To increase interaction among online students, teachers can assign them group projects. Forcing students to work together will add new experiences for the students, and contribute to strong collaboration among them. The most efficient way of learning is group learning. This offers students a chance to support their fellow mates and to learn to work together. Teachers should get the students together in small groups to prepare, and let them and their team create a video project. They may ask them to take photos, record meetings, and upload and complete the project documents, such as pictures or audio files.

Parental Inclusion In Google Classroom

One way to ensure greater parental involvement in Google Classroom learning experience is to organize the evening meetings for the parents and teachers. Teachers and staff can use Google Classroom as a centralized place to book evening appointments for parent-teacher consultation. All instructors are included in Google Classroom, and they can consider the creation of an appointment sheet, when students are given an assignment. In such a form, teachers can book meeting dates with their students, and the school administration would immediately know when the appointment is. This might help make the whole evening coordinated much better and run more smoothly.

It was never simpler to interface with guardians and add parental support in the Classroom, than in the computerized age. Innovation stages offer various approaches to speak with guardians, and this thought is no more peculiar to Google Classroom. There are a few different ways instructors can communicate with guardians utilizing Classroom, yet it is dependent upon the educator to focus on parental contact, and stay up-to-date with the latest class developments and accomplishment of the students.

Schools that utilize G Suite for Education accounts have contact assets that are incorporated into Google Classroom; hence, reaching guardians a simple procedure. Guardians email rundowns and Gmail are two of the most ideal approaches to keep the guardians abreast of what occurs in the Classroom and the achievement of individual students.

Tips to Improve Parental Involvement

Educators and guardians must cooperate to make the students' education fruitful. Unfortunately, parental interest is at a record-breaking low in a few locales. Instructors are continually searching for approaches to battle this, and correspondence is a basic requirement, in my view. Instructors wear a few caps, and they need an answer that is solid to connect productively with guardians. Additionally, since most school spending plans are deficient at best, it is fundamental to discover something that is low or does not cost by any means.

Progress reports

Use Classroom to give progress reports to guardians and students.

Parent forms

Most guardians detest rounding out the heap of structures students' welcome home on a school day. Offer guardians a reprieve by creating on-the-web applications, that can be sent legitimately to the instructor utilizing the Google Applications.

Parent classrooms

Make a Classroom for guardians in particular. Submit applicable archives, and data of schools or classrooms. Submit studies and fundamental dates utilizing the Calendar.§

Target parent phone calls

The reviewing framework offered by Google Classroom empowers instructors to see through to students who are not turning in work. That makes it simpler to follow parent calls.

Here Are Some Tips for Assisting Your Child with Coursework Online

1. Google Classroom can be connected to via an internet browser on a PC, or through a cell phone or tablet gadget.

2. Your perspective on Google Classroom will mirror the assignments that may be missing from your child, or the evaluations that were given out.

3. In the event that you need to see more things that are shared on the online class, make your child sign in to their record with you on a phone, PC, and so on. On the other hand, you can take a look at the course from its point of view.

4. If you are battling to get a grip on any rules for your child's class, do not spare a moment to contact the instructor. This could be their first time running an online discussion, so getting into the swing of things will probably take time. You will all traverse this together!

5. Check the Google Calendar in the event that you experience difficulty in knowing when assignments are expected.

6. Try relaxing.

For some guardians, this is all part of an exceptionally new, strange domain, and numerous educators are likewise attempting to show their children, and they comprehend working all day from home and looking out for their children. Numerous schools are comprehended, on the off chance that it requires a significant stretch of time to become accustomed to new assets and new schedules.

CHAPTER - 10
Google Classroom Tips & Tricks

Google Classroom has become famous for teachers around the world and is being modified continuously. This is why we have agreed to include an extensive collection of beneficial methods you can utilize with your pupils. So, if you are actually utilizing Classroom or just experimenting, read the checklist below and remember how certain applications could work. Need to keep updated on new updates and design changes? Use this handy resource to find out what is new in Classroom every month.

Communication With Guardians And Parents

You can invite visitors to register for a daily or monthly email update of what has happened to at school. The emails include a student's pending or skipped tasks, as well as the notifications and questions you got in the classroom Stream.

Google Calendar Helps Students Stay Prepared

Students can see events like study days and field trips. The Calendar view makes it easy to keep track of this. When new tasks or changes in dates immediately synchronize, the most up-to-date content is still seen by the pupils.

Assign A Task To A Subgroup Of Students

Teachers can assign individual learners or a group of students the job of posting notifications in a class. This function allows teachers to isolate teaching as needed, and also joint support network research. Find the photo below to figure out how that operates.

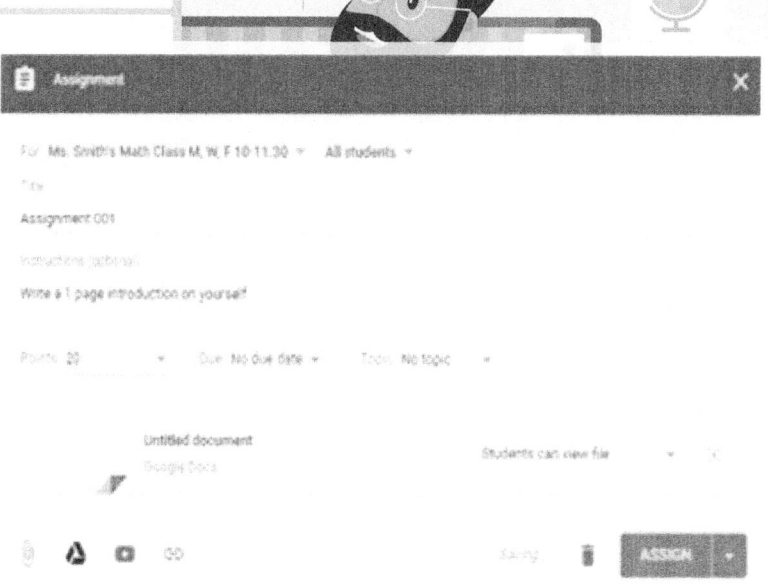

Using Classroom Network Devices With Annotations

The Classroom application will be used by students and instructors using devices with android, iOS, and Chrome. You will have reviews in real-time by annotating the students' work in the application. Learners may also collate their tasks with relative accuracy in conveying ideas and concepts.

Explore Implementation With Other Devices In The Classroom

Google Classroom provides an API to connect with all your key services, and to also exchange them. This puts together hundreds of devices and blogs, including Pear Table, Actively Learn, Newsela, and several others.

Encourage Classroom Metrics For Use By Administrators

While this function is only worth remembering here just for administrators (not learners), managers can use the management console to show statistics, like how many classes have been developed, how many updates have been written, and how often teachers utilize the resources. Exposure to this information can help in customizing training for students.

Fourteen Tips For Teachers

1. Label Your Assignments

Numbering the assignments is one of its greatest ideas I have ever come across. It enables you to not only arrange Classroom files, but to also keep Google Drive clean and tidy.

2. Find The Numbers and Phrases in the Classroom

Only the most organized work in-class page may get very long after a few months of assignments. Use Control + F to search for assignments and knowledge numbers on the page. Teach students the trick, too!

3. Choose Organizational Visions for Themes

The usage of the Topics tab on the Class page allows

us to organize the tasks of students and teachers. There are various ways to become organized. This can be done in several respects; what happens for one instructor does not fit for another. It is a personal preference for students. Select a methodology that fits with your area and material grade point.

4. Create Subject Resources And Keep It At The Top Of A Classwork Page

The class needs a place to put tools, links, rules, syllabus, and other course material. Mindy Barron suggests creating a special content tool and class topic, and placing it at the top for quick access. Make sure that these documents are literally called up, so learners know precisely what is in them.

5. Make a Template for Google Classroom

When you have chosen your ideal form of Google Classroom organization, make copies of a class as your instance. You can make a duplicate anytime you choose a new class, have all your topics already created and organized, and your assignments stored as drafts!

To create a copy of a classroom in Google Classroom, log in to the Google Classroom account, then tap on the three-dotted button of the class card, and pick Copy Lesson.

Go through the article "How To Build A Lesson Prototype" on Google Classroom, for more specific guidance and tips on this idea.

6. Use Direct Mapping Links for Assignments

Maybe you have a direct link to a specific assignment. This makes it very easy to refer learners back to a given lesson. Go to the Classwork tab, find the task, right-click on three-lined button, and copy it.

7. Using Google Docs for Courses

Most learners utilize Google Documents to build a curriculum, so it can be updated as a live document throughout the course of the year. Add external channel links, annual grade quotas, critical times, etc. You may also put ties for Google Classroom projects to prevent getting students reviewed for too long.

8. Split Large Tasks With Different Due Dates Into Smaller Assignments

Task-based education is relevant, so we have to think creatively on how we bring that into practice in the classrooms, as we move past the static, one-and-one activities. Big tasks can be overwhelming for students, especially for those that have not studied how to manage their time. It is important to send them benchmarks and break the mission into smaller tasks with intersections. In fact, this is one of the implementation tips for my novel, Shake Up Education: Practical Tips For Shifting Training From Linear To Dynamic.

9. Establish Special Classes For Extension And Enrichment Programs

Late completion of the task in my class did not mean any spare time or games. This also provided services for my students to read and understand.

Try getting a special section inside online classes for extension or training programs. You may also supercharge the idea, and offer interactive rewards to complete a task or obstacle.

10. Using Personal Messages For Reviews And Conversations With Students

One of my favorite applications on Google Classroom is the Personal Comment button. This simple resource can help streamline interactions with the students, and will improve the feedback loop.

Teacher reviews are a major factor in the development of students! It is just that, personal remarks for both you and the student – own. (No one else can read it.) Note to use private feedback at the conclusion of the mission as well as everywhere else!

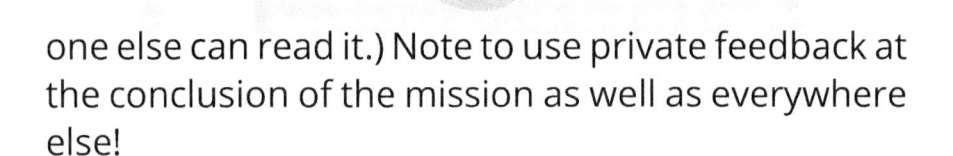

However, it does not eliminate the power of face-to-face sessions, but it does assist documentation. Students can recall the reviews. It also encourages students, who normally do not talk in front of the class, to interact. There are other areas where learners can complement their private reviews.

Click on the task you want to provide comments for, in the Classwork tab, to submit a private message from a Student Worklist. Click the Task View button. From the left-hand roster, pick the pupil. At the bottom of the right-hand column, you will see Post Private Message. Tap to type in a private message. With the new grading function of Google Classroom, you can now even apply private feedback in the student papers.

Tap on the task you want to request reviews from a Classwork page. Tap on the Project Screen window. Click on the student file which you wish to view, using the screen above to render a private post.

11. Using Personal Reflection Comments

Some educators take personal commentary features ahead, and make it a portion of an assignment by enabling learners to add an observation as a personal remark, after submitting their job. Anthony Fahey clearly indicates that you can either use an open-ended query, or offer students a prompt, such as "What do you prefer most about the job?" or "Which part of you is challenged?"

12. For Every Assignment, Attach A Layout Document

In Google Classroom, you can see the Homework tab, and see a preview for each pupil, which helps one to see all the improvement or absence of it at a glance. If you are not using a blueprint for your mission, attach a guide, and you can always get a snapshot of the images.

13. Encourage Teachers Who Are Reluctant To Use Google Classroom

I consider accepting them as a student, at least, because they get a feel of how this functions, so they can join and edit the curriculum as a co-educator. Co-teachers will do something you like within a college. They invite students to take part.

Click on the teacher's Invitation icon to greet you as a co-educator; enter in your username or email login information and click Invite. To invite a teacher as a guest, select the Invite Learners icon, and enter in their title or emails, and then click Invite.

14. Build A Demo Student Account To Display Students In Google Classroom

Google Classroom is not currently giving teachers a way of viewing their courses as a learner. To perceive your school as a student, you must have an account for the student.

The solution guided by Julie Sweeney Thomas is this: using a survey account, log in as a learner to check how Classroom works, and to show how your students can use Classroom. If you have direct exposure to Google accounts within your school's domain, it is simple.

Most teachers are not open to that sort of access. In this case, contact your tech manager or support center to see if you can access a trial account.

CHAPTER - 11
Google Classroom Tips & Tricks

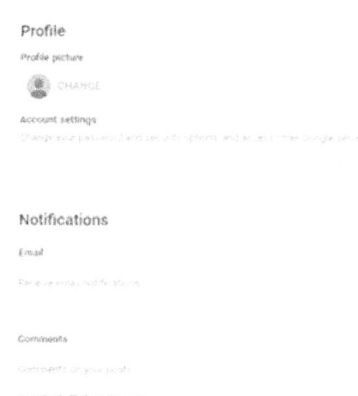

Login Errors

1. You are a teacher using G Suite for Education, but it will redirect you to class as a student. In this case, you need to contact your administrator to assign you the role of the teacher.

2. You are unable to sign into Google Classroom.

You may be trying to log in to a class using an

account for which this service is not available. There are several types of accounts that can be used for progress on the service.

- Account G Suite for Education: It is the official account of your school. It can only be created by formal educational institutions that have accreditation.

- Personal Google Account: It is an account that is created by a student, guardian, or parent of a student. Usually, it is used for private purposes. It can be used for homeschooling or distance learning.

- G Suite account: It is arranged by your organization administrator.

Do not forget to log in to your account; you must connect to the internet.

If you are unable to log in to Google Class using the correct account, the administrator may not have an automatic service activation for new users. In this case, contact your teacher.

Join the Class

I do not remember my password.

If your school uses the G Suite for Education, ask

the teacher to contact the administrator to reset your password.

If you are using a personal Google account that is not associated with an educational institution, reset your password yourself.

Logging out is done immediately for all G Suite products on your device.

In the upper-right corner of the Google Class application, click on your photo. Instead of a photo, there may be a Profile Picture icon.

Select Exit.

Click Logout

Problems with Access to Courses

1. My course code is not valid.

If your school uses the G Suite for Education, ask the teacher to send you a new code. If it does not work either, ask the teacher to contact the school administrator.

If you are using a non-academic personal Google account, ask your teacher to send you a new code.

The code consists of 6-7 letters and numbers, for e.g. g5gdp1.

Note: The course code is only needed to register for the course. It is not required to enter regularly.

2. I do not remember the course code (or the code was accidentally deleted).

If you have deleted, lost, or forgotten the system code, ask the teacher to resend it, or create a new one.

Note: This code is used only once to join the course, it is not required always.

3. I deleted the invitation to the course.

If you cancel the request before joining the class, ask the teacher to resend it.

Note: The invitation to the course is used only for registration. Afterward, it is not required.

4. I left the course but want to re-join.

If you accidentally left the session, ask the teacher to send you the course code or invitation again.

How To Create A Course

If your school uses the G Suite for Education, students cannot create courses.

Issues Related To The Ability To Leave Comments

I cannot leave a comment.

Most likely, your teacher has disabled the ability to post entries in the course feed. Contact him/her for more information.

I Want to Recover A Deleted Entry

It is impossible to recover deleted records, but the teacher can still see them.

Email and Messaging Issues

Unable to send and receive emails.

If your school uses G Suite for Education, your administrator may have disabled Gmail for students. Ask the teacher to contact him.

If you are using a personal non-educational Google account, check out the information in the Gmail

Help Center.

Class Interface Is Displayed In The Wrong Language

How does one change the class interface language?

To do this, you must change the language for your Google account.

Troubleshooting (For Teacher)

Entrance; there may be a problem. Unable to log into Google Classroom.

You can sign into Google Class with the following account types:

- The school account also called the G Suite for Education account.
- Personal Google account that you set up yourself
- G Suite account that is arranged by the organization administrator

If you are unable to log in to the Google Classroom with your G Suite for Education account, the administrator may not have granted you access to this service. In this case, ask the administrator to enable the service in the Google Admin Console.

Below are the error messages that may appear when trying to log in:

Google Class is not available in this account. Most likely, you are trying to log in using a different G Suite account. Log out of your current account, and log in to either your G Suite for Education account, or your personal Google account.

In the mobile application, you will be prompted to add another account. Sign in with your G Suite for Education account or personal Google account.

The system administrator has not activated the Google Class. It means that the Administrator has not enabled the class for your G Suite for Education account. You need to ask the school's system administrator to turn on the Google Class.

I have a teacher account for G Suite for Education, but I enter the class as a student. Ask the administrator to assign you the role of the teacher.

Courses

If you are a teacher at an educational institution that uses the G Suite for Education package, you may have entered the class as a student. Ask your administrator to check whether you are assigned the role of teacher.

Invitations

If you are unable to invite students or teachers to

the course, you may receive one of these errors:

- You cannot invite a student from this domain. It means that you are trying to invite a user from a domain that is not authorized by the administrator. Ask the administrator to change the settings for access to the course in the field.

- You have already invited the maximum number of students. Most likely, you have exceeded the daily limit on sending invitations. You need to ask the remaining participants the following day.

- The list of participants is not available. Most likely, you are trying to invite a Google group, for which the data of participants and their email addresses is not available to you. You should ask the group owner to change permissions.

For more information about adding users to the course, see "How To Invite Students To The Class," and "How To Invite Teachers To The Course."

Tutors using Google Groups may invite students and other tutors to the course. Learn more about creating groups.

Notes

To invite users from a group, it is not necessary to be its owner, but you must be a member. You also need permission to view the list of group members and their email addresses.

Students have problems with course code. If the course code is not valid, you can reset it and give the students a new one. Learn how to reset or deactivate the course code.

Tasks

Is it possible to restore a deleted task?

Deleted tasks cannot be restored, but the files with completed jobs, that students have handed over, remain in the Class folder on Google Drive.

How do I report a problem or send a feature request?

In the lower-left corner of the Google Class window, click the Help (?), then Send feedback.

If you are using a phone on the Android platform, then you need to tap Menu and then Help.

After that, click Submit Feedback.

Enter text, then click on the Send icon to send.

Apple IOS

Click on the Menu icon menu, and then send feedback to Google.

Enter text, then click on the Send icon to send.

GOOGLE CLASSROOM

Email

I cannot send and receive letters.

If you and your students have G Suite for Education accounts, but you cannot use email, your administrator may have disabled the Gmail service. Tell him about this issue.

I cannot invite curators or write them letters.

If you have a G Suite for Education account, but there are no functions in the class to communicate with the student supervisors, try the following:

- Log in to the class through a browser (not through a mobile application).

- Ask the administrator to check whether you are assigned the role of teacher.

- Ask your administrator to permit you to manage newsletters for curators.

Note: If you use a personal Google account to sign in to the class, the link to curators will not be available to you.

CHAPTER - 12
Other Ways Google Classroom Can Help You Succeed

This guide has spent a lot of time talking about the various ways that you can use Google Classroom to enhance all of your learning experience. There may be other programs that are similar and offer some of the same services, but none of them offer these services for free, and none of them have the security and great products that you are able to experience when you are working with Google Classroom. This is really one of the best platforms for all of the needs of teachers and students alike.

In the previous chapters, you learned how to get into a class, how to get setup, and even about how you can share with others in the classroom, to get your work done. You learned how to finish your assignments, and get almost instant feedback from the teacher about what you need to work on to improve your score. Classroom helps you to learn more than you can in a traditional classroom. In addition to some of the things that have been discussed so far in this guide, there are also a lot of other great ways that you can use Google Classroom to make your life a bit easier. Some of the other things that you can consider doing with a Google Classroom account are discussed next.

Google Forms

One of the features that you can do with Google Classroom is to use the Google Forms. These make it really easy for the teacher to obtain information from their students, and for the students to leave some feedback about assignments, the class and more. To keep this simple, the teacher would be able to set up a Google Form in order to open up responses from people in the class. They can ask some open-ended questions, send out a survey, etc. When the student is done with the survey, it will be marked as complete, so the teacher knows when the information is all complete.

Many times, the teacher will use this as a way to provide their students with a survey at the end of the year. They can ask how the class worked, what things they would change, if any, and so on. This is a great way for teachers to keep up with what is going on in their classrooms, and to see if the work is really being that effective.

Google Calendar

The Google Calendar is an automated system, so this makes it easier for students and teachers to keep track of the things that they need to work on, when they are in a particular class. Whenever a teacher puts up a new assignment, project, test or another thing for the students to work on, the due date is automatically going to be placed and synced with the Google Calendar. Students can easily go through and see when their assignments are due for all of their classes, without having to search through all of the classes or spend a lot of time wondering when they are due. The student also has the option to choose to sync the dates that are on their Calendar with their email accounts, or even with their mobile phones, so they can get notifications when the due date is approaching.

Use the About Page

One thing that a lot of students will forget to use is the About page, because they do not think that it is all that important for them. Filling out this About page can be really good for everyone involved. For the teacher, it is a good idea to fill in the About page with accurate information to help the student understand what class they are taking and who the teacher is. For example, teachers may want to consider writing a good description of the particular class, as well as provide links to their website, give information about themselves and their contact information, in case a student needs to get ahold of them.

In addition, students can also go through and fill out an About page as well. They can tell a little bit about themselves to introduce themselves to the other people in the class, share their interests, and so on. Teachers could choose to make this one of the assignments for the students as an ice-breaker, and to help them to learn a bit more about other students.

Reuse The Posts

Teachers can take some of the posts that they used before, in another class or in a previous class, and then reuse them a bit. This can be announcements, assignments, and even questions from their previous classes, to help them keep up with the work, especially if the information still works with this current class.

For the students, it is possible to go through and see some of the old classes that they were in. This can be helpful if you need to review something that is in an older class, or you want to get ahold of some papers or discussions that you want to use from a past semester. You just need to go through some of your past archived classes to find what you want.

Setting The Theme

Some students go into their Google Classroom and leave everything the way that it is. They are happy with the theme and how everything is set up, so they will not want to switch anything around. But if you would like to take your Google Classroom and personalize it, you will be able to do that by changing some of the settings in Google Classroom. There are many different color palettes that you can choose from as well as different themes, so you can test them to find what works the best for your account. In order to set up a new theme that you want to use in the Classroom, you can do the following steps:

- Open Class.

- From here, you can select the Theme button that is at the bottom of the image in Image settings.

- Now you can either select an image from the gallery, or you can click on the Patterns button in order to pick out the theme that you would like.

- Once you have picked out what you would like to have there, you can click on Apply, and the new theme is going to be all set up.

It is also possible to upload some of your own pictures to the gallery in order to use that when picking out the new theme that you are using.

Find Conversation Starters

This is one that the teacher is most likely going to work with, but as a student, you will be able to go through and see what conversation starters the teacher has posted for you. You should be on the lookout for these, to see what the teacher is asking for, such as feedback on the recent announcements, or information about the discussion groups that you need to respond to for a grade. This is a fantastic way for you to keep everyone in the class united, even if they are all in different locations.

Send Emails

Since this is a Google program, you will be able to use the Gmail account to send out emails to other people in the class.

If students need to ask the teacher a question, and they do not want to post it on the open forum or discussion, they are able to send an email to do They can also use their email to talk to individual students or to groups of students who are in the same classroom.

Check Progress

While the student is working on the project the teacher will be able to check how well the student is doing simply by clicking on Submission History. They can then go from here and click on Assignment Status to check the history, to see whether or not the student has been following the guidelines that were set for the assignment, or if the work is just sitting there. It helps the teachers to keep track of who is getting the work done, and who may need a little bit of encouragement. This can hold some of the students accountable.

This is also a good way for the teacher to determine whether they need to provide some extra assistance to their students or not. If they notice that someone has been lagging behind and doing the work but they are not getting very far, they may be able to come in and see if the student needs a little bit of extra help with the assignment. This is a great way to provide some individual help to the student, something that would be almost impossible for the teacher to do in the traditional classroom.

GOOGLE CLASSROOM

There are so many different things that you will be able to do when you are working with Google Classroom. It has some great features that are perfect for both the student and for the teachers as well, which is why this is one of the top reasons that Google Classroom is one of the best in the industry. Learn how to use the various features that are available with Google Classroom, and you are going to see some great changes in the way that students learn, and teachers teach in no time.

CHAPTER - 13
FAQs About Google Classroom

Is It Easy To Get Started With Google Classroom?

Yes, it is really easy to work with Google Classroom, but you do need to remember that it is necessary to have the Google Applications for Education, and your domain needs to be verified.

How Are Applications for Education and Classroom Connected?

To keep things simple, Google Classroom is not able to work without the help of Google Applications for Education. While you are able to use the Applications for Education all on their own, you will find that using Google Classroom is going to help make it organized and much easier to work with. With the help of both the Classroom and Applications working together, both the students and the teachers are able to access the spreadsheets, slideshows, and documents, as well as other links, without having to worry about attachments and more. Even giving and receiving assignments and grades is easier, when these two are combined together.

In addition, there is the option to download the Classroom Mobile application, which will make it easier to access your classes whenever and wherever you would like. This is going to be great for students who are on the go, and do not have time to always look through their laptop to see announcements. Even teachers are able to use this mobile application to help them get up assignments and announcements when they are on the go, so that they can concentrate on other things later on.

Does It Cost To Use Google Classroom?

One of the best things about using Google Classroom is that it is completely free. All you need is a bit of time to help get it all setup, but it will not include any out-of-pocket expenses to make it work. You will have to wait about two weeks in the beginning for your application to be reviewed before you are able to use the class, so consider setting this up early to prevent issues of falling behind.

You will never have to pay for anything when you are using Google Classroom. If you run into a vendor who is asking for you to pay for Google Classroom, you should report them to Google. It is highly likely that this is a fake vendor, so do not work with them or provide them with your payment information. Google Classroom is, and always will be, free for you to use.

Can I Still Use Classroom If It Is Disabled On My Domain?

One of the nice things about working with Classroom is that even if it has been disabled on a certain domain, you are still able to use it. With that being said, there are going to be a few restrictions. While you may still be able to get access to a lot of the features, such as Google Drive, Google Docs, and Gmail, you may not be able to see some of the slides, docs, and sheets that were saved in the classroom. It is always best to have your domain turned on when you are working in Google Classroom, because this ensures that you are able to use all of the features that are available through the Classroom.

Do I Need To Have Gmail Enabled To Use Classroom?

It is not necessary to have Gmail enabled in order to use the Google Classroom. You can use the Classroom as much as you like without enabling

Gmail, but you will find that you are unable to receive notifications if the Gmail account is not turned on. If you would like to have notifications sent to you, you need to have Gmail enabled.

If you are not that fond of using a Gmail account for this, it is possible to set up your own email server to make it work. This way, you will still be able to receive the notifications that are needed from the Classroom, while using the email server that you like the most.

Will I Have To Work With Ads On Google Classroom?

Classroom was designed for educational purposes, and Google recognizes that people do not want to have to view ads all of the time when they are learning. You can rest assured that Google and Classroom are not going to take your information and use it for advertising. This is part of the privacy and security that is offered with Google Classroom, which will protect both the student and the teacher from any phishing or spam.

CONCLUSION

Most of us can recall those moments in our lives when we idly sit in a classroom, but we were not really focused listening to our teachers. Such a scene is still common in school settings these days. This traditional method of learning promoted teacher-centric classrooms and gave less options for students.

We get used to instructors giving us information, students copying what is written on the board, teachers disseminating homework or test papers, and the rest of reading and comprehension improvement will be left to the learners.

Although this traditional method could be effective for some students, many students are forced to be just plain receivers of information, and are not motivated to engage and participate in the learning process.

With the help of technology and the assimilation of various applications, a new learning model has developed. The digital era has penetrated our physical classrooms which removes the teacher-centric method of learning.

Learning has now become more collaborative, and focuses more on student's progress in the classroom. Google Classroom, indeed, is preparing students for the future. We need to know how technology works. Training young students will make them able to communicate and participate to build their future careers. Classroom is helping them become familiarized and comfortable with the technology.

Google Classroom is also increasing student engagement, and keeping students motivated by allowing teachers to motivate them in plenty of ways. Likewise, it gives them the latest information and trends. Web-based content and materials are also accessible to them. Classrooms all around the world can soon be connected to each other, that will broaden information.

For educators, Google Classroom makes it easier for them to deliver instructions while keeping their lesson centered on the students. Now they have more time for discussions and answering questions or conducting problem-solving, instead of doing and checking homework. Students also have adequate amount of time to understand the subjects.

Immediate assistance from the teacher is a must for students to continually grow, and Google Classroom only enhances this aspect. Google Classroom and other learning applications will never replace our teachers, but these tools can help them improve every aspect of learning.

With Google Classroom many teachers have taken the first step to changing how they run their classroom. It is a platform that can be used to help teachers and students alike, and help them benefit from this activity. With Google Classroom, you get the extra benefit of being able to really plan your classrooms effectively, and get students into the spirit of taking their education to new heights. Teachers love this system because it keeps everything in one place. The advent of virtual classrooms and having everything on the computer, has only made learning easier.

Google is coming out with new and improved learning tools as well, such as the tablets that you can get for your students, which help them keep learning. With these additions, along with Google Classroom, your ability to teach the students the core curriculum that they need in order to be successful, is totally possible and worth it.

With that being said, let us discuss the next step that you as an educator, parent, guardian or student

GOOGLE CLASSROOM

should take in order to get the most out of this. For teachers, start to plan your lessons based off this system, and put together the plan. You can from there, with the parents and students, get into this, and you can all keep up with the child's education. Many parents have trouble taking the initiative, but if you have it all together, you will be able to create the perfect scholarly plan for your pupils, and everyone can learn what they want to learn with this amazing system. Learning is being taken to a new, digital future. Google Classroom is providing that, and so much more.

133

Printed in Great Britain
by Amazon